DISPENSATIONAL THEONOMY

The Revelation of God's Law Through the Ages

Jaród Murphey

GLASS MOUNTAINS
PUBLISHERS

Glass Mountains Publishers
820 W Danforth Rd
Unit #476
Edmond, OK 73003

ISBN: 979-8-9933099-5-8

Dedicated to my mother, Raleah,
whose sincere faith in the Lord
and love for the "least of these"
has greatly influenced my life.

2 Timothy 1:5
Matthew 25:34-35

TABLE OF CONTENTS

Chapter I — 1
Introduction

Chapter II — 5
Presupposing the Law of God

Chapter III — 11
Has the Law Been Abolished?

Chapter IV — 17
The Holy Spirit's Role

Chapter V — 21
Two Views of Theonomy

Chapter VI — 29
What About the Ceremonial Law?

Chapter VII — 35
A Third Option

Chapter VIII 43
The Law and the Church

Chapter IX 53
Must Christians Forsake the Old Covenant Law?

Chapter X 57
You Have Reached Your Dispensation

Chapter XI 63
Application to Civil Laws

Chapter XII 69
Personal Application of the Law

CHAPTER I

INTRODUCTION

The law of the LORD is perfect, restoring the soul; the testimony of the LORD is sure, making wise the simple. The precepts of the LORD are right, rejoicing the heart; the commandment of the LORD is pure, enlightening the eyes.
Psalm 19:7-8

Do not think that I came to abolish the Law or the Prophets; I did not come to abolish but to fulfill. For truly I say to you, until heaven and earth pass away, not the smallest letter or stroke shall pass from the Law until all is accomplished. Whoever

> then annuls one of the least of these commandments, and teaches others to do the same, shall be called least in the kingdom of heaven; but whoever keeps and teaches them, he shall be called great in the kingdom of heaven.
> Matthew 5:17-19

For many Christians, understanding verses like these about God's Law is a great challenge. Should we still look to the Law for guidance and keep the commandments as these verses imply? But hasn't the Law been abolished in the church age, this present dispensation? Didn't the Law just apply to Israel in the previous dispensation? So in what sense, if any, does the Law apply to us today as Christians? The study of this topic and these questions is known as *theonomy* (the Greek word for the "Law of God") and is the focus of this short book, which argues that God's Law still has applications for the lives of believers in the church age.

Additionally, this book will present the case that God's Law should serve as the foundation for civil law and governance in any society. At this point, you may be asking some important questions: why is it necessary for a nation to ground its rights and its laws in the Law of God? Isn't it better for a nation to base these things on secular and cultural values? If a nation enforces the entire Law of God found in the Bible, wouldn't that mean Sabbath-breaking and eating pork would be made illegal? This book will answer each of these questions.

CHAPTER II

PRESUPPOSING THE LAW OF GOD

A great scholar of theonomy, R.J. Rushdoony, wrote the following in his book *By What Standard?*

> Basic to this study is the belief that the presuppositions of human thought in every field must be basically one in order to arrive at any concept which both validates biblical faith and human knowledge. The sovereignty of the self-contained God is the key to every field, in that only the God of Scripture makes all things possible and explicable and is thus the basic premise not only of theology, but of philosophy, science and indeed all knowledge. In that God is

> the Creator of all things, He is their only valid principle of interpretation, in that they derive both their existence and meaning from His creative act.[1]

Intuitively, most Christians recognize the truth and necessity of presupposing God's existence and authority in every area. If you ask a Christian why murder should be outlawed, he will (hopefully) answer, "Because God says murder is wrong," and he will be right in saying this.

If, on the other hand, laws should be based on cultural preferences, there is no reason to say the laws in the South which permitted chattel slavery were wrong, since maintaining this system was the preference of Southern culture. If laws should be based on some notion of "human flourishing" driven by societal evolution, then there is no basis to condemn the atrocities of the

---

[1] Rushdoony, R. (1958). *By What Standard? An Analysis of the Philosophy of Cornelius Van Til*. Pg. VII. Ross House Books.

Nazis, who were creating a more genetically-perfect human race by exterminating the disabled and those they deemed genetically inferior, like Jews.

If laws should be based on some religion other than Christianity, which one? In accordance with Islamic law, should wife-beating (Surah An-Nisa 4:34) and the marriage of adult men to six-year-old girls, with sexual consummation of the marriage at the age of nine (Sahih al-Bukhari 5134), be permitted? Should a societal caste arrangement (which forces millions into poverty with no hope of escape) be implemented, in accordance with the Hindu Varna system as required under the Laws of Manu? Should the government require or tolerate sacrificing war captives, poor people, women, children, and babies to appease the gods, in accordance with many pagan religions, like those of the Canaanite,

Aztec, Inca, and Maya civilizations? To avoid genocide, the violation of human rights, and utter insanity, a Christian recognizes that a nation must base its laws and rights on the objective foundation of the Law of God as revealed in the Bible.

Since "theonomy" is the Law of God, a "theonomist" is someone who desires to obey and implement, in all areas of his influence, the Law of God. The area of a theonomist's influence may include family, church, business, nation, government, etc. As Rushdoony put it,

> The man who is being progressively sanctified will inescapably sanctify his home, school, politics, economics, science, and all things else by understanding and interpreting all things in terms of the word

of God and by bringing all things under the dominion of Christ the King.[2]

This sanctification process which Rushdoony speaks of is accomplished by the grace of God and the power of the Holy Spirit, with the end goal of enabling us to perfectly and joyfully obey the Law of God. Greg Bahnsen, another scholar of theonomy, adds,

> The Christian is obligated to keep the whole law of God as a pattern of sanctification, and in the realm of human society the civil magistrate is responsible to enforce God's law against public crime.[3]

---

[2] Bahnsen, G. (2002). *Theonomy in Christian Ethics*. Pg. XII. Covenant Media Press.

[3] Ibid, pg. XXXIX.

CHAPTER III

HAS THE LAW BEEN ABOLISHED?

A foundational scripture in support of theonomy is Matthew 5:17-19, where our Lord pronounces,

> Do not think that I came to abolish the Law or the Prophets; I did not come to abolish but to fulfill. For truly I say to you, until heaven and earth pass away, not the smallest letter or stroke shall pass from the Law until all is accomplished. Whoever then annuls one of the least of these commandments, and teaches others to do the same, shall be called least in the kingdom of heaven; but whoever keeps and

> teaches them, he shall be called great in the kingdom of heaven.

Unfortunately, very few Christians recognize the importance of this passage because of an assumption about what it meant for Jesus to "fulfill" the Law and the Prophets. Many people believe that Jesus fulfilled the Law and the Prophets by obeying the commands found in them perfectly (which is true) and that Christ has imputed His righteousness to us (which is also true), and therefore we do not have to obey God's Law (which is *not* true). A much better understanding of "fulfill" is offered by John MacArthur in his commentary on this passage:

> …Jesus fulfilled the Old Testament by *being* its fulfillment. He did not simply teach it fully and exemplify it fully—He was it fully. He did not come simply to teach righteousness and to model

> righteousness; He came as divine righteousness. What He said and what He did reflected who He is.[4]

As the fulfillment of the Law and Prophets, it would be nonsensical for Jesus to abolish them. Thus, every detail of the Law and the Prophets remain in effect "until heaven and earth pass away." Furthermore, Christians are solemnly warned not to "annul one of the least of these commandments;" rather, they are admonished to fully keep the commandments and teach others to do the same. Even in the New Testament, we are told in passages like 1 John 3:4 that "sin is lawlessness" and, according to Matthew 7:21-23, that fake Christians will be removed from Christ's presence on the Day of Judgement because He never knew them and because they were those "who practice lawlessness."

---

[4] MacArthur, J. (1985). *The MacArthur New Testament Commentary: Matthew 1-7*. Pg. 256. Moody Publishers.

We are instructed to be like Christ (1 John 2:6 and 1 Corinthians 11:1). Since Jesus obeyed the commandments of God perfectly and *is* the righteousness of God, we must strive to obey His commandments (1 John 2:3-5, 3:24, and 5:3) and be perfectly righteous (Matthew 5:48). As Jesus asks in Luke 6:46, "Why do you call Me, 'Lord, Lord,' and do not do what I say?"

CHAPTER IV

THE HOLY SPIRIT'S ROLE

At this point, you may be concerned that theonomists promote works-based salvation. This is not the case. A theonomist believes that a Christian can be saved only by grace through faith. But, according to James 2:17, "faith, if it has no works, is dead, being by itself." If someone claims to be a Christian, but does not do good works, his faith is dead and his salvation is not real. Saving faith is manifested in righteous works. And how do Christians know what righteous works are? How do Christians know how to be righteous in their families, in their workplaces, and in their nations?

According to John 16:7-8, the Holy Spirit is responsible for "convict[ing] the world concerning sin and righteousness and judgment." Although the Holy Spirit can use many different methods to convict us of sin and righteousness, probably the most common tool He uses is the Word of God. 1 Timothy 3:16-17 states,

> All Scripture is inspired by God and profitable for teaching, for reproof, for correction, for training in righteousness; so that the man of God may be adequate, equipped for every good work.

Not only does "all Scripture" include the commandments of Jesus found in the New Testament, it also includes the commandments that He gave as a part of the Law in the Old Testament. Psalm 119:105 says, "Your word is a lamp to my feet and a light to my path." Since the Word includes the Law, it can rightly be stated that the Law of God is a lamp to our feet and a light to our path.

The Law is not found only in the Word of God; it has also been written in the hearts of all men (Romans 2:15). Men know that it is wrong to violate the rights of their neighbors by murdering them, stealing from them, or showing partiality against them, and therefore are without excuse if they disobey God's Law in these areas.

CHAPTER V

TWO VIEWS OF THEONOMY

The preceding chapters presented a rough sketch of the essential foundation of theonomy; but, for those who are interested in a deep study of this area, the books *Theonomy in Christian Ethics* by Greg Bahnsen and *The Institutes of Biblical Law* by R.J. Rushdoony are highly recommended. Although most theonomists will agree on this foundation, there is some diversity of thought regarding how the Law should be interpreted and practically applied today. Currently, the two most popular views on theonomy are the Reconstructionist view and the General Equity view. After briefly describing these two views, I will present the case for a new view, Dispensational theonomy.

The most common understanding of Old Testament Law among Christian theologians is that it should be divided into three categories: the moral law, the civil law (also called the judicial law), and the ceremonial law. Historically, most theologians have argued that the moral law is the only part of the Law still relevant today. It is typically asserted that the moral law consists only of the Ten Commandments. These theologians believe the civil law and the ceremonial law are no longer relevant to Christians. They posit that the civil law consisted of rules which were applicable only to the society and culture in ancient Israel. Furthermore, they believe that ceremonial laws (which includes feasts and festivals, dietary restrictions, cleanliness laws, and sacrifices for sins) were fulfilled and abolished after the crucifixion of Christ.

Reconstructionist and General Equity theonomists both disagree with this mainstream understanding of the Law. They correctly point out that the Israelites had no concept of a division between the moral and civil law. Furthermore, to anyone today who reads the Books of the Law without modern theological presuppositions, to impose this division would seem highly arbitrary. To the open-minded reader of the Old Testament, the entire Law appears to be effective forever. Reconstructionist and General Equity theonomists would agree with the standard view of the law in regards to the ceremonial law. They believe it should be divided from the moral and civil law, that it was fulfilled in Christ, and that it is no longer relevant to Christians.

Reconstructionist and General Equity theonomists differ, however, in how they believe theonomy should be applied today. Reconstructionism, the older school of thought, was first made popular in the mid-1900's by the renowned scholars Greg Bahnsen, R.J. Rushdoony, and Gary North. Reconstructionists believe the Law found in the Old Testament should be applied literally to society today. According to this view, the Law is a blueprint for reconstructing any nation which has strayed from God and for establishing the Kingdom of God on earth.

So, when Deuteronomy 22:8 says, "When you build a new house, you shall make a parapet for your roof, so that you will not bring bloodguilt on your house if anyone falls from it," a Reconstructionist would argue that this law should be applied today in the exact way it says:

nations should have laws today that require new houses to have parapets for their roofs, just like in ancient Israel.

General Equity theonomists, on the other hand, attempt to apply the "spirit" of the Law to today's society. For the General Equity theonomist, the application of the previous verse today would be for a nation to make laws which require roofs, decks, and balconies to have parapets. The spirit of this law dictates that it is evil to have a commonly-accessed high place on your property without a safeguard to keep unsuspecting people from falling and getting hurt or dying. In ancient Israel, people routinely went on top of their roofs and did not usually have decks or balconies; today, it is much more common for people to have a deck or balcony at their house instead of roof-top access. Thus, modern laws should apply to decks and balconies as well. Because General Equity theonomy is more versatile than Reconstructionism, it is the most widely-held view of theonomy today.

CHAPTER VI

WHAT ABOUT THE CEREMONIAL LAW?

The major weakness of Reconstructionist and General Equity theonomy is their understanding of the ceremonial law. Reconstructionist and General Equity theologians correctly point out the lack of a clear distinction between the moral and the civil law in the Law of God found in the Old Testament and that such distinctions are arbitrary. However, after saying this, they attempt to divide the ceremonial law from the moral and civil law. No unbiased reader of the Old Testament would come to this conclusion. In Deuteronomy 12:28, for example, Moses concludes a list of ceremonial law commands and indicates that these laws should be obeyed "forever," when he says,

> Be careful to listen to all these words which I command you, so that it may be well with you and your sons after you forever, for you will be doing what is good and right in the sight of the LORD your God.

Exodus 31:16-17 states,

> So the sons of Israel shall observe the sabbath, to celebrate the sabbath throughout their generations as a perpetual covenant. It is a sign between Me and the sons of Israel forever; for in six days the LORD made heaven and earth, but on the seventh day He ceased from labor, and was refreshed.

Some theonomists argue sabbath-keeping is a moral law. However, its constant connection with the nation of Israel and the fact that the Bible records no pagan nation ever being punished for refusing to keep the sabbath indicates that it is more likely than not a ceremonial law. If that is the case, it is another example of a ceremonial law that lasts forever.

Regarding the placing of blood on a home's doorpost for Passover (an undisputed ceremonial command), Exodus 12:24 says, "And you shall observe this event as an ordinance for you and your children forever." When speaking about the Day of Atonement, Leviticus 16:29 states,

> This shall be a permanent statute for you: in the seventh month, on the tenth day of the month, you shall humble your souls and not do any work, whether the native, or the alien who sojourns among you.

Additionally, in regards to a ritual purification law, Numbers 19:21 says,

> So it shall be a perpetual statute for them. And he who sprinkles the water for impurity shall wash his clothes, and he who touches the water for impurity shall be unclean until evening.

Theonomists correctly point out that it is illogical to say Jesus did not abolish the Law and that His fulfillment of the Law means we no longer have to obey it, but contradict themselves by using this very reasoning to explain why we don't have to obey the ceremonial law. I do not argue that Christians must obey the ceremonial law today; however, this treatment of the ceremonial law shows something is off with how Reconstructionist and General Equity theonomists view the Law. Although these views present an understanding of the Law which is a vast improvement from the traditional approach, they both still miss the mark.

CHAPTER VII

A THIRD OPTION

I propose a new theory of theonomy referred to as Dispensational theonomy. This theory proposes that there are only two laws universally applicable to all of humanity and from which all other laws are derived: love God, and love your neighbor (Matthew 22:37-40). These two laws are objective and universal. But the way these two laws are expressed *sometimes* varies depending on the time period, culture, and dispensation you find yourself living in, in addition to the covenant relationship you and your nation have with God.

To show how Dispensational theonomy should be understood practically, consider an example of primary importance and relevance, the Law of Moses. The Law of Moses was given only to the nation of Israel, not to other nations (Exodus 19 and Deuteronomy 29). This Law contains elements unique to the Israelites, due to their covenant relationship with God. For instance, the Israelites were expected to observe the Sabbath as a sign of this relationship. Exodus 31:13-14 states,

> But as for you, speak to the sons of Israel, saying, "You shall surely observe My sabbaths; for this is a sign between Me and you throughout your generations, that you may know that I am the LORD who sanctifies you. Therefore you are to observe the sabbath, for it is holy to you. Everyone who profanes it shall surely be put to death; for whoever does any work on

it, that person shall be cut off from among his people."

To modern-day Christians who do not understand the significance of Israel's covenant relationship to God, the punishment for Sabbath-breaking sounds intense. However, since the Sabbath is a sign of the covenant relationship between God and the people of Israel, infractions are deadly serious. An analogy may help drive this point home: it is not immoral to remove a ring from your finger and throw it to the ground. By itself, such an action has no inherent significance. But if a married woman who is having an argument with her husband removes her wedding ring and throws it to the ground, this action will be significant and painful to her husband; maybe just as painful as if the woman thrust a knife into him. Why? It is just a ring after all. But the reason this action is significant and painful is because the ring is a sign of the marriage covenant between the husband and wife. In the same way, when an Israelite forsook observing the Sabbath, it was a sign that he had forsaken the covenant between Israel and God.

This is one of the reasons why Christians are not required to obey much of the Law of Moses—specifically, the ceremonial laws. Indeed, the entirety of the Law of Moses was meant solely for the Israelites and their descendants for eternity. But laws which are universally applicable to all humanity are included in the Law of Moses. For instance, adultery, bestiality, incest, and child sacrifice are all forbidden in Leviticus 18. After these and other sins are listed, verses 24-25 say,

> Do not defile yourselves by any of these things; for by all these the nations which I am casting out before you have become

> defiled. For the land has become defiled, therefore I have brought its punishment upon it, so the land has spewed out its inhabitants.

This passage clearly shows it is against the Law of God for both Israelites and Gentiles to commit these wicked acts. Gentile nations were punished in the Old Testament (and are still punished today) for violations of these laws which were universally applicable to all nations. Naturally, they were repeated in the Law of Moses for the people of Israel.

However, there is no record of a Gentile nation being punished for violating the so-called "ceremonial" laws found in the Law of Moses. Sometimes, in the Law of Moses, Gentiles were even specifically exempted from having to follow the same rules given to the Jews. In Deuteronomy 14:21, for instance, the Jews were forbidden to eat animals which had died of natural causes, although foreigners were allowed to. In contrast to the Gentiles, the Jews were punished for violations of these ceremonial laws, the best example being their seventy years of captivity for refusing to keep the sabbatical years (2 Chronicles 36:21).

CHAPTER VIII

THE LAW AND THE CHURCH

As discussed previously, the Law of Moses was given to the Israelites forever and it was never intended *primarily* for the Gentiles. So, if that is the case, are Messianic Jews (Christians who are Jews) still obligated to obey the Law of Moses? Verses like Hebrews 8:13 and Ephesians 2:15 make it clear that the Law of Moses and the Old Covenant are obsolete for those in Christ.

It is important to note here that these references are to the Old Covenant made with the Israelites during the time of Moses (what is spoken of, for instance, in Deuteronomy 4:13). The Covenant made with Abraham on the other hand (Genesis 12:1-3 and 15:18-20), is not obsolete. As a part of this Covenant, God will give Abraham as many descendants as there are stars in the sky and, according to Genesis 15, they will possess all of the land between the Nile River in Egypt and the Euphrates River in Iraq, which has not come to pass yet. Furthermore, Romans 11:17 and Ephesians 2:12-13 make it clear that everyone in the Church, including Gentiles, have been grafted in and inherit the promises of this Covenant with Abraham alongside the physical descendants of Abraham, who have not been forsaken from the Covenant. Romans 11:29 states that "the gifts and calling of God are irrevocable," so this covenant with Abraham is not obsolete.

So how is it that the Mosaic Old Covenant and Law of Moses, which last forever, have been made obsolete? Romans 7:1-6 explains how this works:

Or do you not know, brethren (for I am speaking to those who know the law), that the law has jurisdiction over a person as long as he lives? For the married woman is bound by law to her husband while he is living; but if her husband dies, she is released from the law concerning the husband. So then, if while her husband is living she is joined to another man, she shall be called an adulteress; but if her husband dies, she is free from the law, so that she is not an adulteress though she is joined to another man.

Therefore, my brethren, you also were made to die to the Law through the body of Christ, so that you might be joined to another, to Him who was raised from the dead, in order that we might bear fruit for God. For while we were in the flesh, the

> sinful passions, which were aroused by the Law, were at work in the members of our body to bear fruit for death. But now we have been released from the Law, having died to that by which we were bound, so that we serve in newness of the Spirit and not in oldness of the letter.

In this passage and in Galatians 2:19, Paul makes it clear that because we have died in Christ, who perfectly obeyed the Law, we are not bound to it, whether we are Jew or Gentile. It is not that God has revoked the Mosaic Law or Covenant (God cannot go back on His covenants, which are eternal). Instead, believers have died to this law and this covenant and been joined to a New Covenant.

What is this New Covenant, which is referenced in Matthew 26:28, Hebrews 8:13, and

Hebrews 10:15-17? The New Covenant was promised to Israel in Jeremiah 31:31-34:

> "Behold, days are coming," declares the Lord, "when I will make a new covenant with the house of Israel and with the house of Judah, not like the covenant which I made with their fathers in the day I took them by the hand to bring them out of the land of Egypt, My covenant which they broke, although I was a husband to them," declares the Lord. "But this is the covenant which I will make with the house of Israel after those days," declares the Lord, "I will put My law within them and on their heart I will write it; and I will be their God, and they shall be My people. They will not teach again, each man his neighbor and each man his brother, saying, 'Know the Lord,' for they will all know Me, from the

> least of them to the greatest of them," declares the Lord, "for I will forgive their iniquity, and their sin I will remember no more."

Although this New Covenant was made with Israel and will be fulfilled in its entirety in the future when all Israel will be saved (Romans 11:26), it applies now to all those who are in Christ, including Gentiles (Ephesians 2:11-22 and Galatians 3:27-28). Unlike the Old Covenant and the Law of Moses which could not produce righteousness in those who heard it and instead only condemned them (Romans 3:19-20 and Romans 4:15), in the New Covenant, the Holy Spirit writes the Law of God on the hearts of those who believe in God. More importantly, the Holy Spirit empowers them to obey it (Galatians 5:22-23).

What is this Law, which is written on our hearts? It is the Two Commandments found in Matthew 22:36-40 (love God with all your heart, soul, and mind, and love your neighbor as yourself), as well as a New Commandment which shows how the Two Commandments should be applied for New Covenant people. The New Commandment is described in John 13:34-35, which says:

> A new commandment I give to you, that you love one another, even as I have loved you, that you also love one another. By this all men will know that you are My disciples, if you have love for one another.

This New Commandment is also likely referred to as the "Law of Christ" by the Apostle Paul, who makes mention of it in 1 Corinthians 9:21 and Galatians 6:2. Just like the "ceremonial law" of the Old Covenant did not apply to those outside the Covenant, this New Commandment does not apply to those outside the New Covenant. Unbelievers are not expected to love each other as Christ loves them. There are many other commandments which apply to unbelievers, but that is not one of them. This Commandment serves as a sign for those who are in the New Covenant, allowing everyone to see that those who obey it are part of the New Covenant. In this way, the New Commandment fulfills a similar role as sabbath-keeping in the Old Covenant.

Similarly, the New Covenant includes various ordinances those outside of the Covenant are not required to keep. Some examples include baptism (Matthew 28:19, Acts 2:38, and Acts 18:8), communion (Luke 22:19-20 and 1 Corinthians 11:23-26), and gathering together with the saints (Hebrews 10:25). No one who is outside the New Covenant is expected to obey these commands and there is no record in the New Testament of anyone outside the Covenant being punished for not keeping these commands.

However, there is record of punishment on Christians who do not properly observe these ordinances. In 1 Corinthians 11:20-34, for instance, Paul described how certain believers had "fallen asleep" (a term which is only used to describe the death of believers) because they had taken communion in an unworthy manner. This calls to mind the extreme punishments for those who broke the sabbath. In both cases, violations of these commands are an affront to the Covenant made between God and His people.

Chapter IX

Must Christians Forsake the Old Covenant Law?

A quick note must be added about the Old Covenant before moving on, to avoid placing unnecessary guilt on believers who freely choose to observe ceremonial aspects of the Law of Moses. Some Christians are Messianic Jews who observe Jewish holidays, dietary restrictions, or other elements of the ceremonial law. Although we are dead to the Law of Moses, Romans 14 makes it perfectly clear that it is permissible for believers to still observe the ceremonial law. Furthermore, if their conscience requires them to, it would be sinful if they did not obey these laws. According to the same passage, believers who observe these laws should not condemn those who don't; and those who do not observe them should not despise those who do (Romans 14:10).

Additionally, some believers (both Jews and Gentiles) love and rejoice in the Jewish origins of Christianity and freely choose to celebrate some Jewish holidays or otherwise partake in Jewish culture. There is nothing wrong with this. If Jesus celebrated the Festival of Dedication, Hanukkah (John 10:22-23), it is fine for you to as well. Since the celebration of Hanukkah is not mentioned in the Old Testament—as it was invented after the canon had been completed—we can infer that there is nothing inherently wrong with a Christian celebrating extra-Biblical Jewish festivals in addition to the Biblical ones. Anyone who condemns you for doing this is also condemning the actions of their Savior, who participated in these activities. Similarly, if Paul participated in Jewish purification rituals after the death and resurrection of Christ and after he became a Christian (Acts 21:20-24), you can too. Anyone who condemns you for doing this also condemns the actions of Paul.

CHAPTER X

YOU HAVE REACHED YOUR DISPENSATION

Returning to the main subject of this study, the application of the Two Commandments can vary depending on the dispensation that you live in. According to C.I. Scofield, one of the first authors to popularize the Biblical study of dispensationalism, "A dispensation is a period of time during which man is tested in respect to obedience to some *specific* revelation of the will of God."[5]

During the 4,000 years between the Fall and the death and resurrection of Jesus, mankind was directed to make animal sacrifices as a test of

---

[5] Scofield, C. (1909). *The Scofield Study Bible*. Pg. 5. Oxford University Press.

their obedience and love for God, and to look forward to the future sacrifice of Christ. During this former dispensation, the Two Commandments were applied by offering animal sacrifices, even outside the Covenants and the Law of Moses. Abel and Job, for instance, both made animal sacrifices even though they did not have the Law of Moses and were not part of the Abrahamic or Mosaic covenants. However, in this present dispensation after the sacrifice of Christ, God does not expect or desire humanity to offer animal sacrifices. But, in the dispensation that will begin with the return of Christ, animal sacrifices will again be required, as is vividly described in Ezekiel 40-48. During this future dispensation, the Two Commandments will again be applied by offering animal sacrifices in accordance with the instructions God will give.

Additionally, the application of the Two Commandments can vary depending on the time period and culture you find yourself living in. For example, we are commanded to dress modestly in a way that does not flaunt our wealth (1 Timothy 2:9-10 and 1 Peter 3:3-4). However, the definition of economically modest or immodest clothing greatly varies depending on time period and culture. Oftentimes what is considered economically modest today in this culture would have been considered highly immodest when the New Testament was written. In Roman culture, for instance, wearing purple clothing (which was very expensive to manufacture and typically worn only by royalty or nobility) would have been highly economically immodest; today, however, there is nothing special at all about purple clothing. Two thousand years ago, a Christian who wore purple clothing would have been breaking the Two Commandments; but, today, an American who wears purple clothing is not being disobedient to the Two Commandments.

CHAPTER XI

APPLICATION TO CIVIL LAWS

Although there may be other factors which influence how the Two Commandments are applied, the previous chapters have laid a foundation sufficient for this study. With this out of the way, the application of the Law of God to human rights and civil laws can now be examined. According to Romans 13, governments are given authority by God to bring wrath upon those who do evil. To accomplish this, a nation must have laws that define good and evil behavior, establish basic human rights, and prescribe appropriate rewards for those who do good and punishments for those who do evil. The

Law of God, which is the Two Commandments, must be the bedrock that determines these things.

When magistrates seek guidance on how to create just laws in their nations, including the establishment of human rights, the whole Word of God must be consulted. However, the laws found in the Old Testament will be of particular usefulness. Although the New Testament does have some insight for lawmakers, the main emphasis of these teachings is on the individual, the family, and the church. The Old Testament, on the other hand, places a larger emphasis on the nation of Israel and its civil laws and history, which should be of great interest to rulers and legislators. When considering whether or not a certain behavior should be illegal in his nation, a magistrate should ask a series of questions like the following:

Does this behavior violate the Two Commandments, to love God and love your neighbor?

If so, is this behavior condemned in the Bible?

What is the punishment for it?

Some sins, like pride, malice, jealousy, rejection of Christ, or the refusal of a believer to be baptized or attend church, for instance, are only punished by God (or, in some cases, the Church) and the Bible never instructs government officials to punish these offenses. If the Bible does describe a behavior as sinful and provides for a punishment to be administered by a national government, the lawmaker must also ask if this behavior is only wrong for people groups who are in a specific covenant relationship with God. For instance, if you are a politician in Denmark,

Israelite sabbath laws are not applicable to you or your nation.

These same types of questions should be asked when a lawmaker is considering how to protect human rights in his nation.

To obey the command to love our neighbors, what human rights should we enshrine in our national laws?

Are there specific human rights which are protected in the Law of God or the teachings and examples found elsewhere in the Word of God? If so, we must acknowledge these rights in our laws.

Are there any human rights which, although not explicitly mentioned in the Bible, are in keeping with the totality of the teachings of the Word of God and show love to our neighbors in this present dispensation and culture? If there are, we should also protect these rights in our laws, since the command to love our neighbors as ourselves requires us to do so.

CHAPTER XII

PERSONAL APPLICATION OF THE LAW

A study of God's Law would be incomplete without examining how the Law should be applied in our daily lives and how this differs from the way it should be applied in lawmaking. Unfortunately, when it comes to the Law, many Christians confuse the role they play with the role of the state. For instance, a Christian who correctly understands that evildoers have made themselves the enemies of God and that the state should bring wrath on them may be tempted to treat evildoers in a manner that is rude, dehumanizing, merciless, and sometimes outright hostile. Worse yet, he may try to do the job of the state and enforce the penalty for real or perceived crimes himself.

Christians must remember that the Law of God is applied very differently in their daily lives compared to the role of the state when it comes to interactions with evildoers. If you are a Christian lawmaker, you should be God's minister of wrath against the wicked by writing just laws, and in so doing you love your neighbors in your nation; but, when you interact with an evildoer in your daily life, you should show love and mercy to them and be wise in your interactions with them. You should love them by genuinely seeking their repentance and desiring to do good to them (1 Corinthians 10:24 and Galatians 6:10).

While the Old Testament is especially helpful for lawmakers and voters who desire to make laws that are in accordance with the Law of God, the New Testament is more applicable for learning how to apply the Law in your daily life. In the early church, very few Christians were in the government. Thus, the New Testament does not contain as much practical wisdom for Christian lawmakers who are seeking to apply the Law of God to society as the Old Testament does. However, because the New Testament was written when the New Covenant was inaugurated and the Holy Spirit began to write the Law of God on the hearts of believers, it is overflowing with practical wisdom for how to love God and love our neighbors in every area of daily life.

In the New Testament, we are told in Romans 12:21 to "not be overcome by evil, but [to] overcome evil with good." In Matthew 5:44-45, we are instructed,

> …Love your enemies and pray for those who persecute you, so that you may be sons of your Father who is in heaven; for

> He causes His sun to rise on the evil and the good, and sends rain on the righteous and the unrighteous.

We are admonished in 1 Peter 3:8-9 to "be harmonious, sympathetic, brotherly, kindhearted, and humble in spirit; not returning evil for evil or insult for insult, but giving a blessing instead." In 1 Thessalonians 5:15, we are commanded, "See that no one repays another with evil for evil, but always seek after that which is good for one another and for all people." In 1 Corinthians 10:24, we are instructed, "Let no one seek his own good, but that of his neighbor." And, we are even given a beautiful picture of what love itself should look like in our daily lives in 1 Corinthians 13:4-7, which says:

> Love is patient, love is kind and is not jealous; love does not brag and is not arrogant, does not act unbecomingly; it

> does not seek its own, is not provoked, does not take into account a wrong suffered, does not rejoice in unrighteousness, but rejoices with the truth; bears all things, believes all things, hopes all things, endures all things.

After reading just this small sampling of the wisdom that the New Testament has to offer, no one should come away believing it is okay to dehumanize the wicked, treat them as if they were garbage, or take vengeance on them. If God loves His enemies (Matthew 5:44-45) so much that He died for each and every one of them (1 John 2:2), shouldn't you love them too? After all, He died for you, even while you were sinner just like them (Romans 5:8 and Titus 3:3-7). After you have been forgiven of your great debts, will you act mercilessly to other sinners and treat them as if they are not even humans? Even sinners are made in the image of God and are loved by Him; accordingly, they deserve to be treated with love by you as well.

To conclude this study, I will share some of John Calvin's very moving thoughts on this topic, from his book *On the Christian Life*:

> …We are not to pay attention to what people deserve in themselves but to reflect on the image of God in all people, to which we owe both respect and love. […] Thus, no matter who you encounter who needs your help, you have no grounds for refusing to provide it. Say it is a stranger; but the Lord stamped that person with a mark that should be familiar to you, due to the fact that he forbids you to scorn your own flesh (Isaiah 58:7). Say they are repulsive and worthless; but the Lord points out that this is someone to whom he

has granted the beauty of his image. Say you are not indebted to any service they have done for you; but God has, in a way, presented them as a substitute for himself so that in them you may recognize the many tremendous benefits with which God has obligated you to himself. Say that they are unworthy of even your least effort on their behalf; but the image of God, which commends them to you, is worthy of your handing over yourself and all you have. Even if they have deserved nothing good from you, and not only that, but have provoked you with insults and wrongdoing—not even this is just cause for you to stop embracing them in love and performing the duties of love toward them (Matthew 6:14[-15]; 18:35; Luke 17:3[-4]). You will say, "They deserve something far different from me." But what does the Lord deserve? When he directs you to forgive someone for whatever sins were committed against you, he clearly intends for those sins to be imputed to himself. This is really the only way to accomplish what is not only difficult but utterly contrary to human nature: to love those who hate us, to repay their acts of malice with good, and to reply to curses with blessings (Matthew 5:44). We must only remember that we should not reflect on people's malice but consider the image of God in them, which covers over and erases their offenses and which, by that image's beauty and dignity, draws us to love and embrace them."[6]

[6] Calvin, J. (2024). *On the Christian Life* (R.A. Blacketer, Trans.). Crossway. (Original work published 1550).

www.ingramcontent.com/pod-product-compliance
Lightning Source LLC
LaVergne TN
LVHW090617110826
845146LV00001B/423

* 9 7 9 8 9 9 3 3 0 9 9 5 8 *